sports coach
UK
The National Coaching Foundation

how to coach sports effectively

ISBN 1 902523 52 0

Based on material from *Planning and Practice*
© The National Coaching Foundation, 1984 (ISBN 0 947850 05 8)

Author: Sarah McQuade
Editor: Laura Graham
Sub-editor: Warwick Andrews
Designers: Sandra Flintham and Leanne Taylor
Cover photo courtesy of actionplus sports images
All other photos courtesy of **sports coach UK** and actionplus sports images

Published on behalf of
sports coach UK by

University of
South Wales
Prifysgol
De Cymru

Coachwise
Coachwise Solutions

sports coach UK   Library Service   **Coachwise Solutions**
114 Cardigan Road   Coachwise Ltd
Headingley   Chelsea Close
Leeds LS6 3BJ   Off Amberley Road
Tel: 0113-274 4802 Fax: 0113-275 5019   Armley
E-mail: coaching@sportscoachuk.org   Leeds LS12 4HP
Website: www.sportscoachuk.org   Tel: 0113-231 1310 Fax: 0113-231 9606
                                             E-mail: enquiries@coachwisesolutions.co.uk
Patron: HRH The Princess Royal   Website: www.coachwisesolutions.co.uk

030040

Contents

Introduction

As a coach you will fulfil a number of roles during your coaching practice. Your practice will include a range of styles, behaviours and interactions with participants. What is essential is that you can match your skills with theirs to maximise their learning and to provide a positive sporting experience.

You should recognise that there are different ways of coaching effectively – you may be a live wire or the quiet but firm organiser. Whichever you are, your participants will react to the enthusiasm you bring to the session rather than the loudness of your approach. Remember that, however knowledgeable and enthusiastic you are, the effectiveness of your coaching will depend on good planning and sound practice.

This resource will outline the key components of the coaching process and contains lots of practical tips for you to use in your coaching sessions. Subjects covered include:

- planning and preparing for coaching sessions
- delivering coaching sessions
- evaluating your coaching practice.

- Throughout this resource, the pronouns he, she, him, her and so on are interchangeable and intended to be inclusive of both males and females. It is important in sport, as elsewhere, that both genders have equal status and opportunities.

- Although the emphasis of this resource is on coaching, it is aimed at all those who lead or deliver sports programmes (eg coaches, leaders, teachers, instructors, development officers, officials, administrators, volunteers, parents/carers) and those with responsibility for the organisation of sport (eg national governing bodies, local authorities, centre managers, sports clubs).

Planning coaching sessions

In order to deliver safe, effective and fun coaching sessions for your participants you will have to plan. If you plan your session thoroughly in advance you can ensure that:

- **you give participants the best chance to learn new skills and improve their performance**
- **you make the most of the time available**
- **the coaching environment is safe**
- **you are well prepared.**

How to plan

To plan a coaching session to meet the needs of your participants, you need to know some key information:

- The number of participants
- Their ability level
- Their age range
- The gender mix
- Any specific medical, health or access requirements.

Once you know this type of information, you can start to formulate a session plan. These can be designed in many different ways, but should all contain the same essential information. They are usually designed to help you detail the activities of the session, to reassess goals, plan future sessions and monitor and evaluate progress while you are coaching. You may be familiar with session plans and even have designed your own but a sample plan is shown on page 4 to give you some ideas.

sports coach UK

As a new coach, you might find that you have to put a large amount of detail into your plan so that you know exactly what the activity is, how to set it up and how to group the participants. However, as you become more experienced you probably won't need to complete the plan in as much detail. You might find that diagrams are easier to understand than written instruction and can adapt the format to suit your own style but remember to make sure that other colleagues are able to follow whichever style you choose.

Guidelines for coaching sessions

There are some basic guidelines to bear in mind when planning the content of each session:

- Include a warm-up or preparatory period

- Dedicate time to developing skills and technical ability

- Use a variety of activities

- Select practices appropriate to the participant's ability

- Include a cool-down period

3

sports coach UK

Coaching session planner

Date/time	Venue

Facility and equipment required

Information on participants

Group age	Group size	Ability level

Medical information/particular needs

Session plan

Session goals/objectives		Time
Warm up		
Main activity	Coaching/key points	
Cool down		
Review of session		

Goal-setting

Setting and agreeing goals with your participants is important for their development and progress. Goals also form a fundamental part of your coaching plans and therefore, you should try to establish with each individual what you both want to achieve from the sessions. Make sure that the goals you set are carefully chosen and have a sense of purpose.

Whatever goals are set, they should be recorded and agreed between you and the participant according to the SMART principles. The SMART principles are flexible and you can use them for a specific session or a longer term coaching programme. They are also useful for both group and individual goals that you wish to cover within your coaching sessions.

Specific	Goals that relate specifically to the sport being practised.
Measurable	Goals that can be measured or assessed against a standard.
Agreed	Goals that are mutually agreed between you and the participant.
Realistic	Goals that are challenging and achievable within the participant's ability.
Time-phased	Goals that identify a clear timescale for achievement.

5

Where next?

For further information about goal-setting, refer to **sports coach UK**'s resource A *Guide to Planning Coaching Programmes.*[1]

---

1 Available from **Coachwise 1st4sport** (tel 0113-201 5555 or visit www.1st4sport.com).

What activities to use

Participants need to be given time to practise and learn techniques and skills at their own pace. When deciding how to use your session time most effectively you need to decide when to practise, what practices to use and how often. This decision will be affected by the participants' ability, fitness, age and motivation as well as the type of techniques and skills you are coaching. Also, by recognising how your participants learn, you can create the most appropriate environment to develop skills. You should also bear in mind that practising in a variety of different situations, either simulated or competitive, will assist them in their learning.

You should aim to make your sessions as varied as possible to maintain participants' interest and allow them to develop effectively. A range of suitable activities will already have been devised for your

sport and you should find out more about these from:

- national governing body manuals and seminars
- other coaches
- experienced colleagues within the sport
- participants
- local libraries
- the internet.

Where next?

For further guidance on planning coaching sessions, refer to **sports coach UK**'s resources *Coaching Sessions: A Guide to Planning and Goal-setting* and *A Guide to Planning Coaching Programmes.*[1]

Planning your activities

Having chosen the activities you want to include in a session, you need to plan how best to fit them into the time available depending on the participants and the frequency of your sessions. Practice is

6

described as massed when the rest interval between practices is short or nonexistent. Conversely, distributed practice provides more frequent and longer rest intervals between practice periods – the rest interval is equal to or greater than the practice time.

You can use a variety of methods to allow participants to practise techniques within the blocks of time your session is divided into. You may choose to use **blocked practice** within your sessions. This allows your participants to repeat and refine one specific technique without interruption. It is a useful way to learn specific techniques and is good for beginners but you should progress into more applied practices as your participants' ability improves.

Once the very basic techniques have been learnt, the use of **random practice** is a more effective way to develop skills. By mixing different techniques within your sessions, your participants will become more

involved in their learning and their recall and retention of techniques becomes more permanent.

Constant practice of a technique is where your participants can repeatedly perform one specific technique under the same conditions. This is particularly useful with stable and predictable skills such as archery.

Variable practice is very useful when your participants are becoming more proficient and is an effective way to prepare them for the competitive environment. It differs from random practice in that participants not only perform different techniques but perform them in a different way each time.

Where next?

For further information about coaching new techniques and skills, refer to **sports coach UK**'s resource *Improving Practices and Skill.*[1]

7

---

1   Available from **Coachwise 1st4sport** (tel 0113-201 5555 or visit www.1st4sport.com).

Knowing your participants

Knowing your participants' likes, dislikes and their motivation for being involved in sport can help you to plan your coaching sessions so that their needs are met as effectively as possible. Having this type of information and knowledge will allow you to set realistic goals for them and maintain their enthusiasm for your sport.

Why take part in sport?

Your participants will take part in sport for a number of reasons that may change as they become more involved in your coaching sessions. Recognising their motivation for being involved can help you in providing an enjoyable session for them. They may be there to:

- have fun
- make new friends
- master new skills
- compete and win
- maintain a healthy lifestyle
- become fit.

If participants don't obtain what they are looking for from your sport, they are unlikely to want to stay involved with it. By getting to know them and tailoring the sessions to meet their requirements, you can help them fulfil their potential and get the most out of the sport that has given you so much pleasure.

Motivation can be described as coming from within a person or stemming from outside influences. Participants' internal drive to improve their own performances or abilities for nothing more than personal satisfaction can be described as **intrinsic** or **internal** motivation. You will notice that the most successful performers in your sport often have this basic drive to improve.

Extrinsic or **external** motivating factors include physical rewards such as medals and money or selection for the country or representative team. External motivation can also come from other people but trying to please a demanding coach or parent does not often produce a successful performer.

Putting pressure on your participants is unlikely to motivate them and may even prove counter-productive in the long-term. As a coach, you can help in the motivation process but you should never try to force it to happen.

Whatever their reason for taking part in sport, you can provide the most effective session for your participants if you know more about their reasons for being involved. By developing a good working relationship with your performers, along with their parents, friends, families and teachers, you will be able to identify what motivates them and provide the most appropriate coaching session for them.

Your participant's personality

Besides their reason for being in your session, you also need to understand how each individual tends to behave, helping them to emphasise characteristics such as confidence or leadership and improve any qualities that may affect their performance such as shyness or over-aggression. Their behaviour may alter within different environments such as training and competition. Your role is to help them control any hindering factors such as high levels of anxiety and to optimise factors such as arousal levels before performing.

Personality can influence all aspects of behaviour, from work rate to the way in which participants engage with each other and you during your coaching sessions. Through effective communication (particularly listening) with your participants and seeking to understand their personality and individuality, you can create coaching sessions which are suitable for their needs and that they will look forward to.

Where next?

For further information about mental skills refer to **sports coach UK**'s resource *Motivation and Mental Toughness*.[1]

9

---

1   Available from **Coachwise 1st4sport** (tel 0113-201 5555 or visit www.1st4sport.com).

Delivering coaching sessions

After your planning and preparation is complete, you need to be able to deliver a safe, effective and fun coaching session. Coaching effectively requires you to recognise individuals in the session and to provide the most beneficial and productive experience for them. By creating a safe environment and using coaching styles and methods that suit the participant's needs, you can provide a sound learning environment for all.

Creating a safe coaching environment

Every sport contains elements of danger, some more so than others. As a coach, one of your main responsibilities is to create a safe environment that minimises the risks to participants in your sessions.

Prior to each session, you must conduct a safety check of the environment. By checking all the potential hazards, you can minimise the risk of injury, incidents and accidents occurring in your session. Make sure you check the following key aspects of the coaching environment:

- Facility/venue
- Activity area
- Equipment.

Make sure that the physical environment in which you are coaching (eg hall, outdoor pitch or swimming pool) does not endanger your participants. If the numbers in the group are too large for the space then the activity could potentially be quite dangerous. You also need to consider factors such as floor surface, temperature and lighting.

It is your responsibility to ensure that your participants are made aware of the health and safety guidelines that operate within the coaching environment. At the beginning of each session tell them what the guidelines are and if necessary remind them during the session. Encourage them to read, understand and follow the rules or safety notices and to be safety-minded throughout the session. Make sure everyone knows what to do in an emergency and that first aid is available.

To coach safely, you need an in-depth understanding of the rules and regulations of your sport and an ability to incorporate these into your sessions. The activities that you organise should not place the participants in any danger, either by their content or the way they are set up within the activity area.

Finally, check that the equipment or safety clothing you are using is suitable for the activity and the skill level of your participants. It is crucial to check that everything you need is available and well maintained before the start of the session so that you don't waste vital coaching time when the participants arrive.

Where next?

For further guidance on safe coaching, refer to **sports coach UK**'s resources *How to Coach Sports Safely* and the *Good Practice and Child Protection.*[1]

Coaching style

At the centre of the coaching process are your participants. It is your responsibility to ensure that they are able to make effective choices, discover their own solutions and develop skills at their own pace and in their own way.

As a coach you should use a style within your sessions to maximise your participants' learning. Your style can range from direct instruction and detailed explanation to a facilitated approach, guiding your participants to learn by practising. The style you use is dependent upon the situation, the activity and the ability and preferred learning methods of your participants. The level to which your participants will be empowered to learn may depend largely upon the style you adopt.

11

Effective coaching should be participant-centred, focusing on their needs and abilities.

A participant-centred approach

The coach will:

- share decision making
- share goal-setting and planning
- provide leadership in the form of positive guidance
- encourage participants to share their knowledge and experiences
- allow participants to explore their learning.

A coach-centred approach

The coach will:

- make all the decisions
- direct learning
- closely supervise participants
- present all the information and knowledge.

The style you use may be a combination of the coach-centred and participant-centred approaches and will vary according to who the group is and what they are capable of. You will realise with experience that certain approaches are more suitable for certain types of situations and groups. In the long term, participants who are encouraged to be involved and responsible for their own learning will be better prepared to deal with any situations that arise.

Practical tips

One of the best ways for you to learn is to observe others. Good coaches have a range of styles that they have learnt over a period of time, usually developed as a result of experience as opposed to anything written in a textbook.

Watch another coach in action and consider the following questions:

* What is the age range, size and ability of the group?

* What style do they use?

* Is the coach continually instructing and telling or sharing information and guiding decision-making?

* How are the participants responding? Are they actively involved? Are they performing well? Are they having fun?

* Does the coach's style change when coaching a different group?

actionplus

Developing techniques and skills

Understanding what your performers can do and what they are capable of doing with instruction, guidance and practice should be one of the key principles and features of your coaching. It is your responsibility to structure sessions so that learning can take place effectively.

The terms technique and skill are often used interchangeably. However, techniques are actually the specific movement patterns that participants make during coaching sessions such as kicking or throwing a ball. Skill, on the other hand, is their ability to select and apply the most appropriate techniques to the situation. Put simply, technique is how the movement is performed and skill is when, why and how effectively the movement is applied to the performance.

How people learn

Your participants were not born with sport-specific skills. They will have learnt different physical skills throughout their lives and it is your responsibility to help them improve these and to learn new skills specific to your sport. By recognising how your participants learn and what their sporting abilities are, you can have a significant influence on the outcome of your coaching sessions.

People learn in different ways and your coaching sessions should allow these individual differences to be accommodated.

Kinesthetic learners – people who learn best by practising and exploring actions and movements.

Visual learners – people who learn best from watching others perform skills or visualising actions using pictures or video.

Auditory learners – people who learn best by talking things through and listening to explanations.

Your participants will have their preferred method of learning new skills that may be a combination of the above. What is essential is that you provide good explanations, clear instruction and feedback and use a variety of methods to ensure each participant is able to learn effectively.

A key feature of your role is to empower your participants and to encourage them to be involved in their own learning, a factor that has been shown to improve the learning process. By reflecting on their own performance and that of others, your participants can use that information to continue to develop their skills. They may try other methods to develop their skills, but it is this exploration of the learning process that can enhance their experience within sport. To support this process, you should provide appropriate and safe activities that do not threaten or constrain your participants in their practice.

Whole or part practice?

When coaching a new technique consider whether it should be taught as a whole movement or whether it would be more effective to break it down and teach it in smaller, more manageable parts. The whole practice method is useful for techniques that must be demonstrated or practised as a complete unit. The part practice method is suitable for techniques that can be easily broken down into smaller sub-routines that can be learnt and practised separately before the whole movement comes together.

Techniques taught through part practice can be done in a continuous way where each component is introduced in a logical and progressive sequence, gradually building up to form the whole technique. Participants can also be coached in a progressive style in which each component is isolated and practised before being recombined and practised together.

Your decision on which method to use will depend on the skill you are coaching, how well it can be broken down and the ability level of the group. Whichever method you use, make sure that all participants are able to visualise the skill by giving technically sound demonstrations before they try performing it.

Stages of learning

For whatever skill is being learnt, there are three identifiable stages of learning through which participants will pass on the way to becoming proficient in that skill. To ensure this process is effective you should adapt your coaching according to the stage your participants are in.

Stage one (cognitive stage)
Beginners will devote a considerable amount of effort towards thinking about the movement and building a mental model of how the action is performed. Their movements are often awkward, jerky and unsuccessful and they will not be able to correct their own mistakes although improvements can be rapid with the coach's feedback.

Stage two (associative stage)
During this stage the participants concentrate on practising the skill. Having mastered the skill, improvements in performance become more consistent but gradual. They start to understand how the movement should feel and are able to take on board more complex feedback from the coach in order to correct their mistakes. This stage can last weeks or even months and some participants will never progress beyond this stage.

Stage three (autonomous stage)
At this stage skills are performed without any conscious control or thought dedicated to the mechanics of the movement. Participants can give their attention to the outcome of the movement and to the incorporation of strategies in the game. Participants at this level can detect and correct their own errors and will use their own analytical powers to do this as opposed to relying on the coach.

Practical tips for coaching participants during each stage of learning:		
Stage one	**Stage two**	**Stage three**
• Provide accurate and clear demonstrations. Allow them to develop a mental picture of the movement in action. • Where appropriate break the skill down. Allow them to learn it in logical parts before performing the whole. • Continually praise correct actions. • Give intermittent feedback but don't overload. • Emphasise the process, not the outcome. • Use questions as part of the learning process.	• Break complex skills into sub-routines. • Practise at the game speed. • Encourage performers to analyse own performance. • Don't give external feedback too soon – let them process internal feedback first. • Encourage participants through questioning to analyse their own performance.	• Don't assume learning has stopped. • Focus on finer points of detail. • Practise to maintain techniques. • Draw attention to strategies/ tactics. • Help participants to set new goals. • Encourage mental rehearsal, self motivation and crucially self reflection.

delivering coaching sessions

17

Coaching children?

When coaching children you need to consider their physical development and adapt your practice according to their needs. For further information about coaching children refer to **sports coach UK**'s resources *How to Coach Children in Sport* and *Coaching Young Performers.*[1]

Where next?

For further information about how participants can develop skills, refer to **sports coach UK**'s resource *Improving Practices and Skill.*[2]

Guiding and supporting learning

Throughout your coaching sessions you will provide guidance and support to your participants. Being an effective communicator is a vital skill and one of the qualities of a good coach. The instructions, explanations and demonstrations you use must be presented clearly or your participants will not get the maximum benefit from their time with you.

To guide and support learning you will need to identify the most appropriate way to communicate with your participants. You will need to take into account the nature of the activities, the characteristics of the group and the physical environment in which you are going to be coaching. Choosing the right combination of methods will make the session as rewarding and enjoyable for the participants as you planned it to be.

All the points highlighted in this section combine to promote good practice. If you abide by these guidelines, you will foster a positive relationship with your participants and be effective in enhancing their personal performance.

1 and 2 Available from **Coachwise 1st4sport** (tel 0113-201 5555 or visit www.1st4sport.com).

Effective communication

The key to effective coaching is to provide clear and concise explanations. It is important to think ahead and identify the crucial demonstration and the key coaching points you want to use.

A demonstration is worth a thousand words – provided it is appropriate. If you want to show a particular activity, such as a new game, it may be possible to get a few people playing the game while most of the group continue with the previous activity. When the game is working well, the remainder of the group can be brought round and the game explained while the visual picture unfolds. This avoids those embarrassing delays as the coach tries to get the game going while the whole group watches.

If you are demonstrating a particular technique, make sure the demonstration is basic enough to be repeated by your participants. There is little point in serving like a top professional tennis player if you are trying to show a service that will get the game started for a beginner.

You may also find photographs, charts and models useful to demonstrate a point and you can adapt them to the exact requirements of the particular situation. Video can provide a useful tool to offer feedback and coach techniques or strategies.

actionplus

Verbal explanations to your participants can be one of the most effective methods of communicating. It can be most useful when teamed up with a demonstration; you will be able to make your coaching points clear if you explain them while you or a volunteer actually demonstrates the technique. It is also an effective way to convey tactics or positional play to more advanced participants but you must check that your instructions are clear and that everyone has understood them well enough to translate them into movement.

There may be some occasions when you will need to physically support or guide a participant through a movement or action. This can help participants to understand the movements required to complete a skill. If you are unsure about the guidelines concerning physical support then contact your sport's national governing body to find the most up-to-date information on appropriate ways to give this kind of help.

When setting up your activities you will inevitably give the participants particular aspects of the skill to focus on which are known as coaching points. Don't provide too many coaching points at one time – two or three will avoid confusion or frustration, particularly when coaching children. Use as few words as possible and state these clearly and concisely. Check that the group understand what is to be achieved (particularly organisationally) before they are sent back to the activity area.

Observation and coaching during the activity

The skilful coach is one who can see what is needed next. You can only do this if you step back from the session and let the group get on with it – which they will want to do anyway!

Stand back where you can see everyone, and check that they are all getting on with the activity. From this position it is possible to note a group who have not quite grasped it. Don't rush straight on to the next point – help the hesitant group. Make sure that you keep an eye on the whole group. If you do not do this, you may be helping an individual while half the group have stopped because they have misunderstood the activity.

Keep directing praise, advice or discipline to participants some way off. This keeps the group together, lets the less intrinsically motivated know you are still interested in them, and stops misbehaviour before it can develop.

Remember that you can help a lot without stopping the class – advising them while the activity is going on can be very valuable. Coaching during the activity is a useful skill to learn, and detracts far less from the group's activity.

Providing feedback

By observing each participant during practice and analysing their performance you can then provide feedback. Any errors in technique or skill performance should be noted and appropriate corrective advice given. This advice should be constructive and given

frequently to accelerate learning and reduce the likelihood of practising an incorrect movement.

Feedback to your participants needs to be positive and specific to them and can come from many sources. You can also use the same principles in giving feedback as you would when giving coaching points:

*   Be positive and constructive
*   Don't overload your participant.

Good coaches try to empower their participants and encourage them to analyse their own performance. By using effective questions to aid this self-assessment and reflection, coaches can guide participants in finding their own solutions to improving their performance.

Organising your group

When coaching large groups you may wish to split them into smaller groups to conduct your activities. A fun way to do this, particularly for younger ones, is to get them all to run around your activity area and then rush into a group of the number you call out. A little bit of planning can save time within the session and if participants need to be divided into particular ability groups you will benefit from working out the groups before the session.

The best group size depends on what is to be done in the activity. When organising a piggy-in-the-middle activity in basketball 2 v 1 may be ideal; for beginner hockey players, however, 4 v 1 may be more suitable.

If a session takes the form of starting in sub-groups and building up to a full group, select numbers that allow easy progression. For example, if working in threes it is relatively easy to move to 3 v 3 and then on to 6 v 6 – you merely fuse two groups at each stage. It would be much harder to start in fives, move to 3 v 3 and finish with 8 v 8!

sports coach UK

You can plan a session so that the working area for each person is the same throughout the session. For example, in volleyball you can:

Diagram 1 – 1 v 1 warm-up game

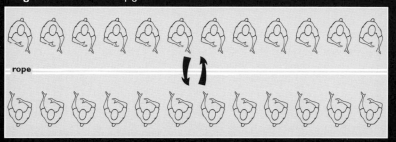

Start the session with a long net or rope down the centre of the hall and organise a 1 v 1 warm-up game as people enter the hall.

Diagram 2 – In threes in one area

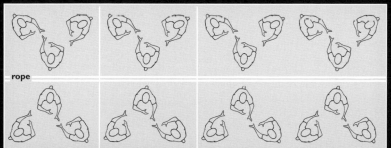

Group the participants in threes and divide them into equal areas, as shown in the diagram, then they are in the ideal position to practise different techniques such as dig, set or spike.

23

Diagram 3 – 3 v 3 across the net

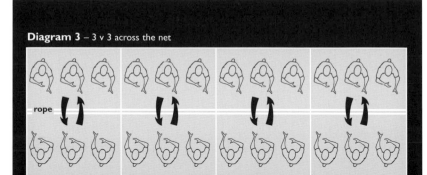

Ask the players to turn to face the group opposite them over the net and practise their techniques in a 3 v 3 game allowing unlimited hits.

Diagram 4 – 6 v 6 across the net

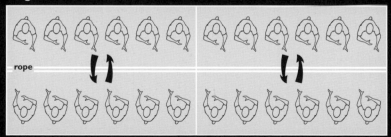

Finally the groups can join their neighbouring group to form a team of six and from here you can organise a 6 v 6 tournament or league.

Stopping the group

Whether selecting sides, organising a competition, explaining a game or giving coaching points, the full attention of the group must be gained quickly, but not oppressively. Even if the group is merely standing around and chatting, they have to be stopped and brought round. There are some essential guidelines to bear in mind when doing this:

- Never stop the group until you know what you are going to say (except for safety reasons). To avoid your instructions being unclear, think precisely about what you want to say before you stop the group.

- Never stop a purposeful activity unless you are sure you have something valuable to say or set up. It is very annoying if a group is getting into something, for them to be interrupted for an irrelevant comment or practice. Don't over-coach.

- Never stop the group until you are in a good position – one in which you can direct your voice to everyone and can see them all – usually to the side of the group.

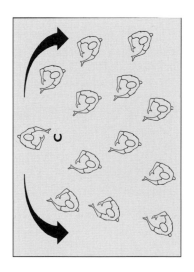

You should modify your positioning a little if it helps you move to a demonstration base. For example, a basketball coach might move down the side wall to a position where, after stopping the group, a few steps take him to the demonstration position X.

In this way the coach avoids a long wait between the 'Stop' and the 'Come round' commands.

- Use one clear word 'Stop', or a whistle. While an experienced coach may use phrases like 'Hold it' or 'OK everybody' to soften the atmosphere, the word 'Stop' is neat and sharp. In large halls with large groups, or if you are soft-spoken, you may wish to use a whistle, but this can be impersonal and does not encourage the lifting of the voice for group control. Try to minimise halts in the activity. Make general points to the whole group, otherwise attend to the needs of individuals without disrupting too many other participants.

- Encourage participants to stop dead when you tell them to and explain why. There are good reasons why the players should stop dead which include safety and saving time. Stopping dead can be encouraged by linking the command to stop with a control skill, such as dribbling a hockey ball. On the word 'Stop' do the groups stop dead? Do the balls stop dead? If they don't, there is the implication of lack of skill, but also a bit of light relief as the ball rolls past the coach.

Bringing the group round

Experienced coaches avoid bringing the group round if their instructions are very brief. Instructions like 'Move into the next activity' in a circuit, 'Remember, not above head height' as a rule reminder, or 'Anyone reaching ten baskets?' as a motivating score check, can be given to a group in their working position without disrupting the activity.

However, if instructions are going to take more than two sentences, or if the hall has bad acoustics, then it is wise to bring the group in. Bear in mind the following guidelines when doing so:

- Direct your voice to the furthest person. As voice control can be difficult to gauge in a large hall, directing your voice to the furthest person (though not bellowing) and checking their response is a good starting point. However, bear in mind also that those in corners to the side of you may be out of earshot.

- Tell participants to 'Stop' and then to 'Come round'. A gesture often helps you indicate what you want them to do. You should also stand so that the group know where to come and do not get behind you. If you prefer to be in the middle of the hall rather than at the side, direct them to come and sit in front of you and stand in a way that makes it clear where you mean.

- Adjust your position to ensure that you can see all the participants. Often a step back brings the entire group into view but if it doesn't, you should not be afraid to ask the one or two who are just out of sight to move. A good check is to see if you can see everyone's eyes.

- If a demonstration is going to occur, the placement of the group will depend on what is to be seen.

- If there is any danger of lack of attention or movement, sit the group down. This is often necessary if your explanation is long or the group is large. It is particularly useful with large groups of active children.

- Think of the equipment they are using and instruct accordingly; for example, tell them to 'Pick up the footballs and come round'. It may help to imagine 30 active 13-year-olds kicking footballs in towards you!

- Decide if the equipment will prove distracting during a demonstration, and instruct accordingly; for example,

'Put the balls in the centre circle and come round'. It is important to avoid being oppressive or finicky, so only tell participants what to do with equipment if you might lose control, and not as a matter of course.

Sending them back

With small groups and adults an informal 'OK' and a gesture may well start the class moving, but with larger and younger groups a more dynamic approach may be helpful. Use 'Go' and/or 'Carry on' to restart an activity. Without these magic words the group does not know exactly when to restart, and therefore may drift away when they think you have finished. With young children, a game in which they wait for the word 'Go', even if you have obviously finished what you wanted to say, has the same appeal as Simon Says.

Timing

You can avoid any wasted time and get the most out of the facilities you have paid for by always starting your session on time, encouraging the group to arrive early and be changed ready to start on the dot. If the first activity is fun and starts on time, you will find the group will be ready and latecomers who have to wait to join in will make more effort to be on time for future sessions. Never start with an activity that requires particular participants, as this is unfair on those who come early, and gives prestige in a way that can be abused.

When the session gets going, be flexible with your time. Your role is to help people and not just to present activities. If a group is a little slow in grasping a new activity then stopping them to move onto your next planned activity when they are just getting interested is both annoying and pointless. It is better to save time on the next phase, or save a practice until the next session. Try to give equal time to all participants, regardless of ability. Don't waste your time acting as a timekeeper within activities, instead give out a timer with a loud bell so they can organise themselves.

Evaluating your coaching practice

Effective coaches are constantly evaluating and improving their performance. Your priority should be to facilitate learning so that your participants' performance improves. In order to progress, it is crucial that you analyse the feedback you receive from others about your performance and use your findings to shape future planning and delivery. By assessing your participants' performance you will also get a measure of how effective your coaching is.

Evaluating participants' performance

Evaluation of your coaching is a valuable element of the coaching process and can often prove to be useful for planning and organising future sessions. An evaluation should be carried out at the end of each session and coaching programme as it allows you to:

- monitor your participants' progress and achievements over a period of time

- compare actual performance gains with anticipated targets or goals

- set future goals and objectives based on the achievements made by your participants

- select teams

- assess whether your coaching sessions are appropriate

- assess your ability to coach.

Keeping a record

In order to measure your participants' improvement you will find it useful to keep a written record of their performances, perhaps using a shorthand code or a specially designed record sheet. You can collect information on technical and tactical aspects such as patterns of play or set pieces and also physical and mental aspects such as training loads or behavioural characteristics. Through continued monitoring of your participants' performance, you can help analyse performances in comparison to those of previous training or competitive environments.

29

Using video

Video footage can be one of the most valuable methods of evaluating your participants' performance as it allows them to watch themselves in action. By using freeze frame you can isolate any technical faults that have been made and run through them in slow motion with the participants while giving coaching points. You should choose occasions to use video wisely however, as it can be expensive and sometimes time consuming when working with a large group.

Performance tests

You can use performance tests to monitor and evaluate performance of skills, fitness levels or even personality type. There is a variety of tests that you can use but make sure the ones you choose:

- provide useful information which will help you and your participants to improve their performance
- measure what they state they will measure

- are reliable and would produce the same results if repeated
- are objective and would produce the same results regardless of who the tester is
- are carried out according to standard procedures
- are appropriate to the age, ability and experience of the participants.

Where next?

For further information on performance testing, refer to **sports coach UK**'s resource *A Guide to Field-based Fitness Testing.*[1]

Ask the participants

The best way to gather information about how your participants feel they are progressing, what may be holding them back and whether the sessions are beneficial to them is to ask for their opinion. You could conduct a

[1] Available from **Coachwise 1st4sport** (tel 0113-201 5555 or visit www.1st4sport.com).

simple question and answer session at the end of the session or programme or distribute a questionnaire if you want to study their views at length and in more detail.

Questionnaires should not be too long and the participants should understand their purpose. The information will only be valid if their responses are honest so take into account that some participants might give you the answers they think you want as opposed to what they actually think or feel. To avoid confusion, make sure that the questions are clearly worded and unambiguous and relate specifically to the content of the session, their rate of learning and their personal goals.

By communicating with your participants you can evaluate the effectiveness of the activities you use to aid their learning and whether you are using the right style and guidance. If you find that participants are not achieving, improving or enjoying your sessions then you may want to consider delivering parts of them in a different way.

Where next?

For further information about motivation and goal-setting, refer to **sports coach UK**'s resource *Observation, Analysis and Video.* [1]

Evaluating your own performance

Once you have an idea of how your participants are performing you should reflect on your own performance by asking yourself and others how you are doing. Having delivered your coaching session or programme there are a number of questions to consider regarding aspects of your planning and delivery; you can only evaluate your own performance effectively if you ask yourself the right questions and make sure you are not overly self-critical.

The Coach Analysis Checklist in the Appendix is a useful tool to find out how effective your coaching is. You either fill it in yourself or get a colleague who has watched you coaching to complete it; you can even use it as a feedback form for participants. Study the answers you get back carefully and compare them to your own. You will no doubt get some invaluable feedback in terms of your strengths and weaknesses and which areas you should be working on in your own personal development.

actionplus

Where next?

Coaching is primarily about developing people through the sporting context. By providing a safe and ethical environment where your participants are able to fulfil their potential, you can continually assess and improve both your participants' performance and your own.

You should aim to make your coaching as effective as possible by preparing and planning your sessions in advance and by using safe and appropriate activities to develop participants' learning. Your coaching style may change according to the participants and environment in which you coach, however, you should always try and coach in a way that will benefit their learning and personal development. To continue providing effective sessions you should constantly evaluate your coaching to ensure your sessions remain fun, safe and effective at all times.

Many of the points in this resource will continue to be valid throughout your coaching career. They are skills to be built up over several years. Your continuing education as a coach will only benefit your participants if the knowledge and skills you have gained are put into practice in an effective way.

sports coach UK (scUK) offers a variety of workshops and resources related to effective coaching.

Workshops

- Coaching Methods and Communication
- Goal-setting and Planning
- How to Coach Sports Effectively
- Improving Practices and Skill

For more information about these workshops, contact your nearest Regional Training Unit (RTU). RTU contact details are available from **scUK** (tel 0113-274 4802 or visit www.sportscoachuk.org).

Resources

The following resources are available from **Coachwise 1st4sport** (tel 0113-201 5555 or visit www.1st4sport.com):

- Galvin B and Ledger P (1998) **A Guide to Planning Coaching Programmes**. Leeds, The National Coaching Foundation.

- Crisfield P, Houlston D and Simpkin A (1996) **Coaching Sessions: A Guide to Planning and Goal-setting**. Leeds, The National Coaching Foundation.

- Foxon F (1999) **Improving Practices and Skill**. Leeds, The National Coaching Foundation.

- Cabral P and Crisfield P (1996) **Motivation and Mental Toughness**. Leeds, The National Coaching Foundation.

- Robertson K (1999) **Observation, Analysis and Video**. Leeds, The National Coaching Foundation.

Other resources in the Coaching Essentials series[1] include:

What is Sports Coaching?
This new resource clearly defines coaching and introduces the basic components of coaching sessions. Including sections on the roles, responsibilities and qualities of a coach, it is an ideal introductory text for new and existing coaches. (Based on *The Coach in Action*.)

How to Coach Sports Safely
Focusing on safe practice in sport, this resource outlines the health and safety issues associated with coaching. Includes new sections on managing risk and manual handling. Essential guidance for every coach. (Based on *Safety and Injury*.)

How to Coach Children in Sport
Aimed at anyone working with children in sport, this easy-to-read title presents the basic principles of good practice and introduces the concept of long-term athlete development. (Based on *Working With Children*.)

---

[1]   Available from **Coachwise 1st4sport** (tel 0113-201 5555 or visit www.1st4sport.com).

How to Coach Disabled People in Sport

This introductory text tackles all the frequently asked questions posed by sports teachers, coaches and participants about how to work with disabled sports people. As well as a whole spectrum of new ideas for inclusion, the text will introduce and offer guidance to any coach involved with disabled people in sport. (Based on *Working With Disabled Sportspeople*.)

Useful contacts

sports coach UK

sports coach UK (scUK) works closely with national governing bodes to provide a comprehensive service for coaches throughout the UK. This includes an extensive programme of workshops which have proved valuable to coaches from all types of sport and every level of experience. For details of **scUK** workshops in your area, contact your nearest Regional Training Unit. For more information about **scUK**'s workshops and other services, contact:

sports coach UK
114 Cardigan Road
Headingley
Leeds LS6 3BJ
Tel: 0113-274 4802
Fax: 0113-275 5019

E-mail:
coaching
@sportscoachuk.org

Website:
www.sportscoachuk.org

National governing bodies

Senior coaches in your sport have a wealth of experience and knowledge to offer. If you do not know a senior coach locally, contact your sport's governing body for further advice.

The national governing body for your sport or activity will give advice on coaching courses and other relevant information. National governing body contact details are available from:

> **Central Council of Physical Recreation**
>
> Francis House
> Francis Street
> London SW1P 1DE
> Tel: 020-7854 8500
> Fax: 020-7854 8501
>
> **E-mail:**
> info@ccpr.org.uk
>
> **Website:**
> www.ccpr.org.uk

Appendix

Coach analysis checklist

The following statements may help you evaluate your coaching. Read each statement and tick the accompanying box if you agree with them when applied to your coaching. If you have not ticked the box this may indicate areas that you need to work on and you should try to establish reasons why and use this information to action plan for the future. Remember, even if you have ticked a box you may still need to review your practice in this area. If you decide that you could improve on this, then think of how you can do it for your next coaching sessions.

When coaching techniques and skills, do you:	Tick
Use language and terminology that the participants understand?	
Speak clearly?	
Gain everyone's attention?	
Face participants when speaking to them?	
Make good eye contact with them?	

When coaching, do you:	Tick
Use verbal instruction?	
Provide accurate demonstrations?	
Use both verbal instruction and physical demonstration together?	

38

When demonstrating, do you:	Tick
Direct all of the participants' attention to the demonstration?	
Demonstrate the whole skill as it would be performed in competition?	
Give both right and left handed demonstrations?	
Demonstrate the skill several times?	
Demonstrate the skill at different speeds?	
Demonstrate the skill so that it can be viewed from different angles?	
Keep explanations simple and brief?	
Give three relevant coaching points to focus on?	
Repeat and answer questions so that all can hear?	

During activities, do you:	Tick
Use activities that allow the performers to practise safely?	
Demonstrate and explain how the activity works?	
Check that participants understand how the activity works?	
Use activities that focus on the skill being taught?	
Divide the skill into parts when participants can't master the whole skill immediately?	
Provide explanations and demonstrations to correct errors?	
Stop practice and correct common errors?	
Use a variety of activities in the session?	
Concentrate on the same skill for the whole session?	

When providing feedback, do you:	Tick
Observe and evaluate performance?	
Compliment efforts and parts of the skill that were performed correctly?	
Correct one error at a time?	
Give specific, positive and constructive feedback?	
Ensure that participants understand the information given?	
Show patience with participants?	
Encourage participants to continue to practise and improve?	

39